CW01045942

Consistent Christian Living

4 Keys to Remaining in Victory

Yan Hadley

New Life Publications

Published by New Life Publications
45 Heatherbrook Road
Anstey Heights
Leicester LE4 1AL
Tel: 0116 2356992

Copyright © 1997 Yan Hadley

All rights reserved. No part of this publication may be reproduced, stored in any retrieval system, or transmitted, in any form or by any means, electronic, mechanical, photocopying, recording or otherwise, without the prior permission of the publisher.

Short extracts may be used for review purposes.

Unless otherwise stated all Scripture quotations are from the Revised Standard Version of the Bible. Copyright © 1946, 1952 by the division of Christian Education of the National Council of the Churches of Christ in the United States of America.

A V- Authorised Version. Crown copyright.

NIV- The Holy Bible, New International Version. Copyright ©1973, 1978, 1984 by International Bible Society.

ISBN: 0 9531107 0 2

Typesetting, Design and Production by: KingFisher
Charis House, Hardwick Square East, Buxton, SK17 6PT

❖ Dedication ❖

This book is dedicated to all who have so faithfully supported this ministry and ourselves as a family, over many years. Also, to those very special individuals who throughout my life have been a constant inspiration and encouragement. Their kindness and sensitivity to me, especially in times of adversity, has proved their true friendship and has been of incalculable value.

❖ Contents ❖

❖ Acknowledgements ❖

My grateful thanks go to my wife Lorrainne, for all her patience and hard work in typing the manuscript; often from notes that were not always too legible!

Much appreciation is also due to Helen Cockram in Cheshire, Dr Paul Goffin in Leicestershire, and Pastor Steve Moss in Lancashire. Their diligence in carefully proof reading the text has been a tremendous help.

❖ Introduction ❖

"In the world you have tribulation; but be of good cheer,
I have overcome the world." (John 16:33b).

Realism about life's trials, yet confidence regarding our triumph is how Jesus presented the challenge of the Christian life. This same balance sums up the book you are about to read. In following Christ there will be hazardous turns, stormy seasons, as well as detours in discouragement and weariness, causing our path to be difficult. However, God has made every provision necessary to enable us to live consistently for His glory, which is *"normal"* Christianity. We don't have to be disappointed by our attempts to live steadfastly. Nor need we be frustrated as we receive God's blessing one day, only to find that the enemy of our souls has snatched it from us the next. Rather, we can discover and apply the key principles found in God's word to every circumstance of our life and remain victorious.

Most people have a bunch of keys in their pocket or handbag somewhere, which are a variety of shapes and sizes. It is self evident, that the size of the key is relatively small compared to the object that it is able to open up. This is so, whether you think of a padlock, your car door, or the front entrance to your house.

The same is true with the key principals of God's word and is what this book seeks to share. What could change our lives might only be a short verse of scripture, perhaps some simple aspect of truth, or even just one word. As we by faith though, apply that key principal to our situation, it is able to open up to us a life far bigger and greater than we ever imagined. The principles shared in this book can release us into a new confidence and enable us to remain walking in victory. They will help us to realise our full potential as we enter into a new dimension of living.

◆ FIRST KEY ◆
STEPPING BEYOND SORROW

It has been said of the German Composer Georg Friederich Handel that when his health and finances were at a low point, he rose to the greatest heights of his creative experience. His creditors were threatening him with imprisonment, and he was suffering from partial paralysis. He then went into seclusion and there drew near to the Lord as never before. During that time God enabled him to write the grandest of all his choral works, *Messiah*. The notes seemed to fly from his pen.

What a marvellous fact it is, that in spite of the problems which may come against us, as Christians we are able to move from the place of sadness, to the place of song! This is why the gospel is the most positive message in the world. It enables us to have a personal testimony so that with confidence we can say, *"God does care, He will answer prayer, and He still works miracles today!"* The gospel is relevant to our every need because, *"Jesus Christ is the same, yesterday and today and forever."* (Hebrews 13:8).

While speaking at a meeting in Manchester recently, I noticed a lady in her eighties, two rows back from the front, in considerable pain. She was talking to the people beside her, and weeping with discomfort. At the end of the service she asked for prayer, saying that she had severe arthritis throughout her right arm and leg. This was the result of an accident over three years ago, when she fell off a moving bus into the road. She could hardly move her arm or leg and needed the aid of a stick to walk.

As we prayed together the healing power of God came upon her. Immediately she was able to vigorously lift her arm up and down, without any restriction. She then raised her right leg without any pain, walked without her stick and even began to dance! Full of joy she testified to the people around her and then said to me, "Yan, I'm not going to need my stick any longer and when the health visitor comes to visit me, she's going to get a real shock!" Only fifteen minutes earlier she had been in great pain, weeping, but now she was laughing and rejoicing at what God had done!

As I think of this miracle, the words of scripture come to mind and show us why we should confidently expect to remain consistent in our Christian life, even when there are times of difficulty. God's word says, *".... Weeping may tarry for the night, but joy comes with the morning."* (Psalm 30:5).

In focusing on this truth, let us consider the following areas that enable every Christian to step beyond sorrow, into singing and live consistently.

Firstly, - THE PAINFUL CIRCUMSTANCES

The scripture says, *"Weeping may tarry ......"* Christianity is certainly not for "softies." Jesus not only told us, *"the gate is narrow,"* which we have to enter through, He also said, *"the way is hard."* (Matthew 7:14). We have never been guaranteed a problem-free life. In fact when you look at those in the Bible who accomplished anything for God, you'll notice they were people who went through times of great trial. Take Job for example; after thousands of years, the name Job still stands as a testimony today, even to the unconverted. The unbeliever may know nothing whatsoever about the Bible, but they've all heard of the name Job and understand that it is synonymous with suffering, patience and endurance.

When Job commented on life, his conclusion was very clear. He said, *"..... man is born to trouble as the sparks fly upward."* (Job 5:7). Right from birth, the one thing we can be sure of is the inevitability of suffering. The words of the Psalmist also come to us with just as much realism. David says, *"Many are the afflictions of the righteous*

......" (Psalm 34:19). This verse wouldn't be so bad if it said, *"one or two afflictions,"* or if it was referring to the rebellious and ungodly. It is stating however, that those who love the Lord and are serving God as best as they know how, can expect *"many"* afflictions. Having faith in God certainly doesn't make us immune from trials.

The apostle Paul, commenting on his own life and ministry says, *"We are afflicted in every way."* (2 Corinthians 4:8). Also, Peter adds a practical word of counsel to the Christians who had been dispersed and exiled in Pontus, Galatia, Cappadocia, Asia, and Bithynia. These believers were going through painful circumstances. They needed to be strengthened and encouraged to remain consistent in their faith, so Peter writes, *"Beloved, do not be surprised at the fiery ordeal that comes upon you to prove you, as though something strange were happening to you, but rejoice in so far as you share Christ's sufferings......"* (1 Peter 4:12&13).

We hear about situations every day of pain, tragedy and sadness and know from our own experience that life at times can be very cruel and people less than kind. Circumstances can begin to overwhelm us and events suddenly take us by surprise. Just last year I was due to be speaking at a church in Lancashire, but the day before the meeting the pastor said he would have to cancel the service. He explained that three members of his church had just been involved in a serious car crash and the wife of one of the leaders was in a critical condition, on a life support machine! These people never imagined as they began that day and got into their car, that there were going to be any problems, but life is like that. When we least expect it, something can suddenly happen to throw us into turmoil.

For us all, though perhaps in a less dramatic way, difficult circumstances strike and have the potential of shaking our faith. For some, it might be the pain of a bruised or broken relationship; for others the concern and burden they have for a rebellious son or daughter, or maybe an unsaved partner. In other cases it might be conflict and difficulty at work, the pressure of a financial struggle, the strain of ill health, or possibly the unkind words and thoughtless actions of another against us.

The scriptures give us plenty of examples of weeping and also reveals the causes of such sorrow. These areas are universal reasons for distress and are just as common today as they were in the Bible. They are:

(A) *Guilt and Shame:*

The cause of King David's sorrow was due to the fact that he was convicted of his unconfessed sin. In Psalm 32:3&4 he says, *"When I declared not my sin, my body wasted away through my groaning all day long. For day and night thy hand was heavy upon me."* If at any time we try to hide our sin, or pretend that it isn't that important, we not only deceive ourselves, but also lose the joy and fulfilment we used know.

(B) *Bondage and Oppression:*

Great sorrow and torment had come upon Israel because for so many long years, they had been held captive in Egypt. God said of their situation, *"I have seen the affliction of my people who are in Egypt, and have heard their cry because of their taskmasters; I know their sufferings......"* (Exodus 3:7). Many people find themselves in situations where they feel bound and oppressed, struggling with circumstances, or habits that have enslaved them emotionally, mentally, physically and spiritually. Because they have not stood firm they have come under the yoke of bondage that Paul warned Christians of when he said, *"For freedom Christ has set us free; stand fast therefore, and do not submit again to a yoke of slavery."* (Galatians 5:1).

(C) *A Desperate Need For A Miracle:*

This was the cause of Hannah's suffering and heartache. She was desperate for a miracle, just as many are today. She wanted her hopeless situation of childlessness to change, for God to reverse what seemed irreversible. The Bible says of her emotional turmoil, *"She was deeply distressed and prayed to the Lord, and wept bitterly."* (1 Samuel 1:10).

(D) *Demonic Attack and Discouragement:*

The activity of Satan and his demons in attacking the lives of Christians is just as real today as ever it was. This was the affliction that was wearing Job down. He said, *"My face is red with weeping, and on my eyelids is deep darkness."* (Job 16:16).

(E) *A Deep Sense of Failure and Regret:*

This is exactly what we see in Luke 22:62. Because Peter had just denied the Lord, we read, *"he went out and wept bitterly."* How often we also make great claims and resolve to do so much, yet when the crunch comes, find ourselves not living up to the good intentions we had. Our response to the challenges of life, at times, falls far short of the sincerity of our convictions.

(F) *Disappointment and Confusion:*

I'm sure many can identify with the cause of Mary's tears. She couldn't understand why things had turned out in the way that they had. Her brother Lazarus had just died and although Jesus could have helped, He didn't appear to do anything. Her request, just like our prayers and needs at times, seemed to have gone unanswered. Mary's sorrow is evident in the words, *"When Jesus saw her weeping, and the Jews who came with her also weeping, he was deeply moved in spirit and troubled."* (John 11:33).

Having looked at the variety of painful circumstances, some of which we can no doubt identify with, lets consider now an additional pressure that tries to break our resolve to live consistently:

Secondly, - THE PROLONGED WAITING

This is the hard one that affects so many Christians today; the time between the problem we have and the promise of God being fulfilled. The waiting period can be very difficult to accept. This is why we need to look at Psalm 30:5, specifically where it says, *".... Weeping may tarry for the night ..... "*

I'm sure we've all experienced at some time that restless night, when we just can't get to sleep, no matter how hard we try. In fact the harder we try, the more difficult it is to find any sleep. We just lie there in the darkness, endlessly waiting for morning to come. Almost always things appear worse in the darkness. The night seems endless, our worries feel greater, the problems look bigger, our fears grow stronger and we feel so alone.

That same uncomfortable feeling can be experienced spiritually in the darkness of our painful circumstances; the feeling where is God? Why doesn't He do something? There are times when God can seem a million miles away. This was how Job felt; in all his pain and weeping he was searching for God, but the Lord seemed nowhere to be found. Job says, *"Behold I go forward, but he is not there; and backward, but I cannot perceive him; on the left hand I seek him, but I cannot behold him; I turn to the right hand, but I cannot see him."* (Job 23:8&9).

In this push-button, computerised, instant age in which we live, people are conditioned to expect everything right away. When instantly our prayers aren't answered and automatically the breakthrough doesn't come, it can begin to affect us if we are not careful. This is why Solomon wrote, *"Hope deferred makes the heart sick......."* (Proverbs 13:12). When there is a period of delay,- impatience, doubt, frustration, hardness and even anger towards God can creep in. Delay can introduce the nagging uncertainty, "Will my prayer ever be answered?" "Will my situation ever change?"

A few years ago, I was speaking to a Pastor of a church in Leicester. He was sharing a particular burden he'd got with regards to his twelve year old daughter. Since the age of nine and a half she had suffered from a fear of vomiting. It was a totally irrational phobia, but so strong in her life, she was unable to attend school, or play outdoors. She even had great difficulty going to the shops with her mother. This resulted in her being placed into a special clinic for those suffering with Anorexia. The pastor said to me that the situation had brought a great strain upon their marriage and family life and he had stepped down from leadership of the church because of it. Then in exasperation he said, "It's been two and a half years now and sometimes I wonder whether it's ever going to change!"

The effect the waiting period has upon a person, can bring them to the place of despair, where all they've previously believed in begins to crumble. This is why the Bible says, "..... *by sorrow of heart the spirit is broken.*" (Proverbs 15:13). As the situation begins to eat away at a person's faith, the consistency that was once so strong is shaken to the point where they almost give up expecting any breakthrough to come.

Sometimes it is hard to understand why the answer is delayed in coming. Indeed, when we read John 11:5&6, it is very hard to grasp the logic, because it says, *"Now Jesus loved Martha and her sister and Lazarus. So when he heard that he was ill, he stayed two days longer in the place where he was."* Jesus deliberately delayed when he heard about the crisis. Rather than immediately responding to the situation, He chose to wait.

This doesn't seem to make sense. However, if we are to remain consistent in faith we must believe that God is never late and His timing is always perfect. Behind the delay there is a divine purpose that often isn't seen in the short term, but is revealed eventually. For example, in this story of Lazarus, we get a glimpse as to why Jesus waited and the purpose behind the delay. Jesus says to His disciples, *".... This illness is not unto death; it is for the glory of God, that the Son of God may be glorified by means of it."* (John 11:4). Then again in verse 14&15 we read, *".... Lazarus is dead; and for your sake I am glad that I was not there, so that you may believe."* I can't imagine anything more glorifying to the Lord, or faith building for the disciples, than to see a dead body being brought back to life again!

One of the most important lessons I've learnt, from personal experience, about the waiting period is, don't wait *passively* for something to happen, wait *actively!* For example, in the waiting period there are three things that are vital for us to do. These are:

(A) *Declare In The Darkness What You Believed To Be True In The Light*

Rather than getting negative in the things we say, we must guard our words carefully and be sure that we maintain a positive confession of faith. The things we believed, without a shadow of doubt, when everything was going well and we had no problems, we need to speak out and declare in the dark and difficult times.

(B) *Decide To Keep Busy In The Work Of The Lord*

The great temptation, when our prayers don't appear to be answered and no change seems to be coming, is to begin to let things slide. For example; not to be so regular at meetings as at one time we were, not so fervent in prayer, or diligent in God's word, not as enthusiastic in praise and worship, or quite so keen in evangelism. During the waiting period, 1 Corinthians 15:58 is crucial, it says, *".... be steadfast, immovable, always abounding in the work of the Lord...."*

(C) *Determine In God's Strength To Rise Above The Disappointments And Set Backs*

Life is full of disappointments and if we want to achieve anything for God there will be a lot of set backs. Unless we determine that we are going to rise above these, then we will always be restricted in our potential and find ourselves kept down by the power of Satan.

Having considered the painful circumstances and thought about the prolonged waiting the next area to look at is:

Thirdly, - THE PROMISED BREAK THROUGH

Ultimately, the only way we can bear the waiting, is when we *"know"* that the breakthrough is certain to come! This is why verse 5 of Psalm 30 is so important. It says, *".... Weeping may tarry for the night, **but joy comes in the morning.**"* As surely as night is followed by day, just as sure is it that the darkness of our painful circumstances are going to change! Maybe not in the way we want, or when we think they ought to, but change is absolutely certain!

No matter how deep the darkness may seem, the "night" is a fixed period of time, with an end to it. For some it may be hours, for others days, weeks, or months; but we must dwell on the truth that hallelujah the morning is coming!

God's word makes a very definite promise for those who don't give up and who will not rush ahead of Him, trying to make things happen in their own ability. For people who will wait with faith in God's faithfulness we read, *"..... those who wait for the Lord shall possess the land."* (Psalm 37:9). We will enter into all that God has provided and experience everything He has promised, as we wait for Him to act. The same assurance is given in Isaiah 49:23. Here the Lord says, *".... those who wait for me shall not be put to shame."* We will never be found among those who walk around with their faces to the ground, shaking their heads, thinking, "Why did I ever believe and expect my situation to be any different?" If we will wait for Him, He will not allow us to be put to shame by anyone!

When daybreak arrives in the natural realm, after we've been waiting endlessly in the darkness, it's always such a great relief. We tend to feel, - "At last the night is over!" - "At last the morning has come!" This was very much the case for a woman from Ashford in Kent, who came out for prayer some years ago. She had been waiting and weeping a long time, for her situation to change. As she shared her circumstances she said, "Will you pray for me, because I desperately want a husband and there just doesn't seem to be any possibility of that at all."

She made it clear that she didn't want "any old man," she wanted a man of God, someone who loved the Lord. "Please pray," she said, "because I don't want to be left on the shelf." Well, we prayed together and asked God to provide. Some time afterwards I had a letter from this woman and she said, "Yan, it's wonderful! Since you prayed I've had two proposals of marriage and I'm getting married next year!" One of the sentences in her letter read, "From the moment you prayed, it took God eleven months and two weeks and He's done it!"

There is a light therefore, that will always break through the darkness, bringing reassurance and security. The Bible says, *"Thy word is a lamp to my feet and a light to my path."* (Psalm 119:105). Also, in verse 130 it says, *"The entrance of thy words giveth light....."*(AV). We need to get God's word into our emotions, our thought life and into our circumstances, so that as Jesus taught, we live by, *"....every word that proceeds from the mouth of God."* (Matthew 4:4). When we hear, respond and walk according to God's word, we let in the light of God's power to drive away the darkness of doubt, disappointment and despair!

Now as we think of the importance of God's word to our lives, let's consider:

Fourthly, - PRINCIPLES THAT STRENGTHEN CONFIDENCE

If we are to live consistently, overcome the things that confront us and take hold of every opportunity that presents itself, we need strong confidence. This is available to all who will commit themselves to the following principles:

(A) *Maintain A Right Relationship With God*

This is the very foundation of all our confidence. The Bible says, *"Beloved, if our hearts do not condemn us, we have confidence before God."* (1 John 3:21). If we have confidence to stand before a holy God, we will always have confidence to face whatever confronts us in life. This means though, that we must of necessity, keep short accounts with God and with our fellow man, so that there is no cloud of unconfessed sin over our life.

We see in the Bible how this was the foundation that Job's life was built upon. In all his pain and prolonged sorrow, the one thing he knew without any doubt was that he had a right relationship with God. Job could say, *"But he knows the way that I take; when he has tried me, I shall come forth as gold. My foot has held fast to his steps; I have kept his way and have not turned aside. I have not departed from the commandment of his lips....."* (Job 23:10-12). What a tremendous example, of someone who lived by every word that proceeded from God's mouth.

(B) *Disregard Whatever Contradicts With What God Has Said*

As we seek to live consistently there will be many occasions when our feelings, circumstances, rational thinking and the opinions of others will try to undermine our confidence in what God has spoken. It might be in relation to a prophecy over our life, or a promise that we've held on to; maybe some direction we've received, or assurance we've been given.

The tactic of Satan is always to weaken our confidence and his strategy goes right back to the Garden of Eden. The way he sought to break man's relationship with God then, and snatch away his confidence, was simply to whisper, *".... did God say, "You shall not eat of any tree of the garden?"* (Genesis 3:1). And also in verse four, *".... You will not die."* It was because Adam and Eve did not disregard what they were hearing that disaster struck and their consistent walk with God was destroyed.

We need to learn to be more like Abraham of old. When God's word came to him, saying that he was going to be a father in his old age, not just of one child, but a great nation, he believed God's word. The Bible says, *"He did not weaken in faith when he considered his own body, which was as good as dead because he was about a hundred years old, or when he considered the barrenness of Sarah's womb. No distrust made him waver concerning the promise of God, but he grew strong in his faith as he gave glory to God, fully convinced that God was able to do what he had promised."* (Romans 4:19-21).

To come to this place of strong confidence Abraham had to disregard his own body and the barrenness of his wife, who was ninety years old herself. He also surely had to disregard the reaction and opinions of others, who must have laughed at the very thought of him ever becoming a father at his age!

(C) *Rest In The Assurance That God Is In Control*

When we truly accept that God is still on the throne and is ruling over every situation, it gives us strong confidence. We can know a peace that passes all understanding because we are convinced that, ultimately, He is in charge of our destiny. Nothing will ever take God by surprise and never for one second will Jesus Christ ever stop being Lord!

We don't have to be anxious, or come under undue pressure, because when we believe in the almighty power of God, we know that even the things that Satan intends for evil, God is able to turn and work for good! This is why the Bible says, *"Thou hast turned for me my mourning into dancing....."* (Psalm 30:11). Only God could ever do that! Not the psychiatrist, or psychotherapists, but God alone. Just look at the extreme contrast in the verse we've just mentioned. The place of mourning is one of darkness and despair, a feeling of utter hopelessness and helplessness. God, however, is able to transform mourning into dancing!

When you think of the darkest moment in the history of the world, it surely must have been when Jesus hung suspended between heaven and earth upon Calvary's cross. The Bible remarks of this time that, *".... there was darkness over all the land."* (Matthew 27:45). As you imagine in your mind's eye this awful occasion, what a picture of apparent defeat and failure; of apparent weakness and humiliation, yet the Bible says, God raised Christ Jesus from the dead, then, *"..... highly exalted him and bestowed on him the name which is above every name."* (Philippians 2:9&10). Therefore, from the depths of such apparent defeat, to the heights of such glorious victory God turned the situation around.

What this means for you and me, and why we should have such strong confidence, is that no matter how impossible the situation we're facing might seem, or how helpless we might feel, God is able to reverse any circumstance. Believing this to be true, enables us to rest in faith.

(D) *Trust That The Lord Is With You, In Spite of Your Feelings*

Our emotions, if we allow them, will rule our life. This is one of the major causes of inconsistency in the lives of Christians. Feelings will tell us when to read our Bible and pray; when to go to the meeting; when to praise the Lord and how much we should give in the offering etc. It is because people allow their feelings to dictate to them, that they fail to maintain a strong testimony, continuing to walk in God's blessing and victory.

We need to trust that the Lord is with us, even though at times it doesn't feel like it. His promise says, *".... and lo, I am with you always, even to the end of the world."* (Matthew 28:20, AV). The confidence that we have as Christians will be proportionate to our trust in this truth. This is why the writer to the Hebrews wrote, *".... For he has said, "I will never fail you nor forsake you." **Hence we can confidently say,** "The Lord is my helper, I will not be afraid; what can man do to me?"* (Hebrews 13:5&6).

There will be occasions in our life when we find ourselves going through the most unexpected trials. Even in these periods though, when we trust that the Lord is with us, we will maintain our faith. This is why God spoke through the prophet Isaiah to encourage and reassure His people. He said, *"When you pass through the waters I will be with you; and through the rivers, they shall not overwhelm you; when you walk through the fire you shall not be burned and the flame shall not consume you."* (Isaiah 43:2).

Another threat to our consistency, where our feelings tend to throw our life into a complete turmoil and our enthusiasm goes right "out the window," is when we feel hurt by the words, or attitudes of another person against us. This tends to cause our resolve to weaken and feelings of discouragement and disappointment to overwhelm us. However, the assurance of God's word, particularly at such times, makes all the difference. The psalmist knew about this from personal experience when he wrote, *"The Lord is near to the broken-hearted, and saves the crushed in spirit."* (Psalm 34:18).

(E) *Continue To Call Out To Him, Knowing That He Will Respond*

We should take encouragement from Psalm 30:2. It says, *"Oh Lord my God, I cried to thee for help, and thou hast healed me."* The mistake we often make is that we pray about a situation once or twice and when it's not automatically answered we think, "Well that's it, it can't be God's will. I've just got to accept the situation." Perhaps we'll come forward for ministry in a meeting with our need and when nothing appears to happen we feel, "Maybe this is my cross to bear and after all, other people's needs are greater than mine." In thinking like this we find ourselves accepting situations that God never intended us to have.

We give up far too quickly and in doing so our unbelief is exposed. We need to be more like Bartimaeus, the blind beggar. In all his darkness and sorrow, when he heard that Jesus, the answer to his need, was passing by, he was determined not to give up. He called out from his darkness, knowing that this was the only way his problem was ever going to change. When the crowd heard him, they told him to keep quiet. They considered him to be an embarrassment and there was no way Jesus would be interested in him. He could so easily have felt hurt and rejected at this rebuke. The temptation for him to give up must have been very strong. He could easily have thought, "Perhaps they are right, Jesus wouldn't be concerned with my need." The Bible tells us though, that when Bartimaeus heard them say those words, *".... he cried out all the more, "Son of David, have mercy on me!"* (Mark 10:48). The result was, Jesus heard his cry and met his need.

(F) *Share Your Burden With Someone You Can Trust*

Our confidence is strengthened when we open up our lives to others, rather than keep the problem "bottled up" and suppressed. Too often people wear masks of pretence. Perhaps someone will say, "How are you today?" and we reply, without thinking, "Fine thank you very much, praise the Lord!" This is because we dare not let anyone know the issues we are struggling with, because we feel that they would consider us *"unspiritual"* and less of a Christian.

Each one of us are in the same position! We all have problems and issues that we've got to work through. Because of this, God has given us one of the most powerful and beautiful things He could ever give, to strengthen us in times of difficulty, and that is "fellowship." The Bible says, *"Rejoice with those who rejoice, weep with those who weep."* (Romans 12:15). Also, *"Bear one another's burdens, and so fulfil the law of Christ."* (Galatians 6:2). Sharing with others we trust, who can strengthen, encourage and pray with us, can bring tremendous reassurance into our lives.

The miracle that happens when just one other person comes into our situation of need is quite amazing and brings great strength to our confidence. The Bible says, *".... A threefold cord is not quickly broken."* (Ecclesiastes 4:12). When there is God, ourselves and one other Christian to stand with us in faith, we will not easily be shaken. Also, we find the Bible teaches that when just one other person comes in to support us, supernatural power is released from heaven to answer our prayer. Jesus said, *"..... If two of you agree on earth about anything they ask, it will be done for them by my Father in heaven."* (Matthew 18:19).

Painful circumstances in life are therefore very real, nobody would deny that. Also, the prolonged waiting is extremely hard, but praise God that the promised breakthrough is absolutely certain! While we are waiting for our prayer to be answered and our need to be met, we must make sure that we don't wait passively, kept down by the situation, but we wait actively as we live by the principles of God's word. In doing so we will be able to step beyond **Sorrow** and into **Singing,** regardless of our problems.

⬧ SECOND KEY ⬧
STANDING IN LIFE'S STORMS

It was a horrifying and traumatic experience when, at the age of seven, Glenn Cunningham and his older brother were badly burned in a school fire. Sadly his brother died, and the prognosis for Glenn was poor; in fact the doctors thought he would never walk again. However, such was the tenacity of this young boy that he refused to accept their verdict. As time went by, Glenn made good progress and not only walked but began to take a keen interest in athletics.

He worked diligently in training, overcoming disappointments and setbacks, then eventually entered the 1932 and 1936 Olympic Games, winning a silver medal in the 1500 metre race. Glenn was the fastest miler in the Amateur Athletic Union every year but one between 1933 and 1938. In 1934 he astonished the spectators by running a mile in 4.06 minutes, - a world record that remained unbroken for three years.

To a greater or lesser degree, all runners must overcome pain and hardship if they are determined to achieve their goal and finally win. In the same way, overcoming and remaining steadfast through trials is also essential for every Christian. It is necessary that we are continually reminded, not only to rise up out of our problems, but resolve to stand firmly at all times.

Storms, as we've made clear in the previous chapter, are events in life we all face, no matter who we are. It is the strong winds of adversity and billowing waves of difficulties that try to stop us living consistently for God. They arrive with unnerving regularity, often strike without warning and linger without welcome. The good news is though that whether those storms are physical, emotional, or spiritual, the ability to overcome and stand victorious in our circumstances, is possible.

Jesus gave the same call, linked to a promise of blessing, to each of the seven churches in Revelation chapter two and three. It was a promise dependant on them "Conquering" in their particular situations and is just as relevant for us today. As far as the Lord is concerned, He expects those who believe in Him to be "Overcomers!"

In looking at Matthew 8:23-27 we find some helpful lessons that enable us to live consistently and remain strong in any storm. Here it says, *"And when he got into the boat, his disciples followed him. And behold, there arose a great storm on the sea, so that the boat was being swamped by the waves; but he was asleep. And they went and woke him, saying, "Save, Lord; we are perishing." And he said to them, "Why are you afraid, O men of little faith?" Then he rose and rebuked the winds and the sea; and there was a great calm. And the men marvelled, saying, "What sort of man is this, that even winds and sea obey him?"*

The phrase in this passage that immediately stands out to me, is the last part of verse 27 *".... And the men marvelled."* It is wonderfully true that, **Whenever God Moves, Man Marvels!** We see this in the Old Testament, as, miraculously, God moves in impossible situations, revealing His glory and greatness. This is also evident in the New Testament. As God moves, healing the sick, raising the dead and driving out demons, man just stands in awe and wonder at what He is able to do.

This fact still remains true today in the 20th Century, in spite of all our sophistication and technology. When God supernaturally moves upon people, they look in amazement at what He is able to do. An example of this that I witnessed not long ago was in the life of a very aggressive and explosive man from Bacup in Lancashire. He was twenty stone, six feet tall and would often fly into fits of uncontrollable rage at the least provocation. By throwing chairs around in the meeting and using bad language as well as threats, he was able to intimidate people in the church there. On more than one occasion this man had threatened to "break the legs" of those that he was angry with!

As I was preaching in the meeting this person came and sat on the back row staring intensely at me. At the end of the service, he immediately came forward and asked to see me, *"Out the back!"* So with wisdom being the better part of valour, I took two other men along and we went into a side room. To our surprise, he said God had challenged him and he wanted to repent of his hardness of heart and sinful actions. I invited him to pray in repentance first, then we prayed for God's Holy Spirit to move in his life. As we did so, the power of God came upon him, he fell back against the wall and just slid down till he was flat out on the floor! When eventually he got up again, he was as quiet as a lamb and looked a changed person! It was very reassuring then, as it is now, to be reminded that no storm is bigger than God, nor stronger than His power!

In reading from Matthew chapter eight, there are three aspects of this story that enable us to be consistent regardless of whatever we may be confronted by:

Firstly, - THE SECRET OF SURVIVAL

To get through life today, with all its pressures and conflicts, we need to know how to survive. Unless we do so, we shall most certainly find ourselves "sinking" under the pressure of the storm.

(A) *"Alertness":*

This is one of the first basic principles of survival. We need to make sure that we are not taken by surprise and caught off guard. Whenever we are not alert to the possibility of a threat we are at our most vulnerable. This is why Peter taught, *"Be sober, be watchful. Your adversary the devil prowls around like a roaring lion, seeking someone to devour."* (1 Peter 5:8).

If we were informed that a lion had escaped from a nearby circus and had just been seen in the vicinity of our house, I'm sure as we stepped outside, we would be 'twitching' nervously, looking all around with keen alertness. This would be so because we'd take seriously the threat of a literal lion! We need as Christians to take seriously God's Word in this respect and become more guarded to the attack of the enemy on our lives. Not that we should ever nervously be afraid of Satan, paralysed with fear of his attack, so that it causes us to be inactive and anxious of the repercussions of serving God; far from it. Paul says in Ephesians 6:18 we are to: *"..... keep alert with all perseverance..."* We need to be vigilant, yet at the same time remain busy, persevering and pressing on in the Lord's service.

Often the attack to our life will come, when we least expect it. Perhaps immediately following a time of personal victory, sense of achievement, or great blessing. This was the case with Elijah in 1 Kings 19. It was because he was not alert to the storm that came against his thoughts and emotions that right after his incredible triumph on Mount Carmel, he came crashing down to defeat, running away in panic for his life.

Another time when the storm comes, taking us by surprise, is when we are not doing what we ought to be doing, or when we are relaxing away from the "battle field." For example, when we're away from the eyes of the Church and our spiritual guard is lowered. This was the cause of King David being in a position where he fell to the temptation of lust with Bathsheba, that we read of in 2 Samuel 11. A man after God's own heart was brought down to such depths because he was not alert to the danger he was in!

In Matthew 8, the reason such fear and panic came to the disciples was because they were taken by surprise. The Bible says, *"And when he got into the boat, his disciples followed him. And behold, there arose a great storm on the sea, so that the boat was being swamped by the waves...* " (verse 23&24). It must have been wonderful to follow Jesus when miracles were being performed and thousands were flocking around to hear his teaching. They never imagined though, that to follow Jesus on this particular occasion, might result in the loss of their lives!

There aren't many things that are certain today, but one thing is absolutely sure; when we follow Jesus and get into His boat, storms will soon blow up. Following Christ means that either you will hit the storm, or the storm will hit you! It might be storms of conflict and persecution against our witness, or tension and strife in relationships. Maybe the storm of fear and doubt, physical sickness, financial pressure, or possibly anxiety and worry about the future. Whatever the storm might be, we need to keep alert because God's word says, *".... the enemy shall come in like a flood...."* (Isaiah 59:19, AV).

(B) *"Attitude":*

The next basic principle of survival relates to how we see our predicament. In the midst of the storm we need to have a positive view of the situation and refuse to allow ourselves to be overwhelmed by the pressure of our circumstances. We need to believe that we are going to make it through the difficulty! This attitude is taught by Jesus when He said, *".... In the world you have tribulation; but **be of good cheer**, I have overcome the world."* (John 16:33). Storms can give us the opportunity to overcome and prove God, or we can let them be the barrier stopping us getting across to the other side. A wrong attitude will always prevent us from getting to where God wants us to be.

The encouraging certainty is that Jesus wants us **all** to get across to the "other side." From the place of where we're struggling, to where we are standing in confidence and strength. From the side of defeat to that of victory. From despair to hope; from sickness to health; from bondage to liberty; from failure to success, and from sadness to joy. In fact whatever situation we may be in that appears negative, the Lord wants us to get across to the side of the positive promise of His word! In Matthew 8:18 Jesus gave a command for His disciples to, *".... go over to the other side."* If only they'd had the attitude, "Well Jesus has said it, so that is what's going to happen," then things would have been very different for them.

The disciples could not have been in a more secure place. In fact, they were in the safest location on the face of this earth. There was no way the boat could sink, no possibility they were going to go under, because the Lord of all creation, who upholds all things by the word of His power, was in that same boat! Now if they'd had that attitude, they would have remained confident even in such an apparently critical situation.

(C) *"Action"* :

We should never just lay down and accept anything and everything that life, or the devil throws at us. Never allow a defeatist, apathetic response to hinder us living consistently for the Lord. The Bible says, *"Submit yourself therefore to God. Resist the devil and he will flee from you. Draw near to God and he will draw near to you."* (James 4:7). In each of these directives, action is required on our part. Too many people are robbed of victory and fail to maintain their stand for God because they have been worn down and brought to the place of thinking, "There is nothing I can do about the situation, I've just got to accept things as they are!"

Several years ago, I was sitting in the home of a man from Devon who had come to this state of despair in his life. Everything seemed to be against him and though he was a Christian, his circumstances had worn him down to the place of feeling hopeless and helpless. As we talked together I began to pray for him, then suddenly, part way through the prayer, God gave me a prophetic word to speak into his life. It was something I'd never heard, or thought of before, but it was absolutely right for him. The main substance of this word was, "You must begin to assert your will, release your faith and choose to be a victor rather than a victim!"

Since that time, as I've pondered on that statement, it has become so clear to me how this truth will set anyone free, no matter what storm they may be in. To **Assert Our Will** means that we've got to begin to take action by rising up inside and refuse to accept the lies, doubts and fears that the enemy is trying to plant into our mind. It's as we take responsibility to do something about the way that we're thinking that it begins to be the first step in changing our life. This is why the scripture says, *".... take every thought captive to obey Christ."* (2 Corinthians 10:5). And again, in Romans 12:2 we read, *"Do not be conformed to this world but be transformed by the renewal of your mind...."*

Then we need to, **Release Our Faith.**- The only way to release faith is to act upon what we believe to be right. James says, *".... faith, if it hath not works, is dead."* (James 2:17, AV). It's as we start to speak out the truth of God's word and begin to do what we know to be right, even though we may not feel like it, that God's power is activated to uphold us. The time that we least feel like praising the Lord, is when we most need to do so. When we don't feel like going to Church, that's when we've got to make sure we're there. It's on occasions when we'd rather not read our Bible that we must discipline ourselves to do so. In the storm of emotional turmoil and difficult circumstances, we must do what we know to be right. A good example of this is the Psalmist, when he was feeling discouraged and depressed he spoke to himself and said, *"Why are you cast down, O my soul, and why are you disquieted within me? Hope in God; for I shall again praise him, my help and my God."* (Psalm 42:5).

The final part of action required on our part is to, **Choose To Be A Victor, Rather Than A Victim!** - Very often people have a victim mentality when things begin to go wrong for them and this only escalates their problem. It is no good when we're in the storm, thinking, or feeling , "Why does this always happen to me?" - "There's no way out of this situation!" - "It's hopeless!" We need to choose to be a "Victor," because, in reality, that is exactly what Christ has given us the ability to be. As a result of His provision the Bible says, *".... we are more than conquerors through him who loved us."* (Romans 8:37). Also, *"Thanks be unto God, who always causes us to triumph in Christ."* (2 Corinthians 2:14, AV). It is not a case therefore of mind over matter, or simply the power of positive thinking. It is choosing to believe and act upon the truth of God's word, even when our circumstances or feelings may seem to tell us otherwise.

The next aspect of the passage in Matthew chapter eight is:

Secondly, - THE SOURCE OF OUR STRENGTH

This is vital to consider, because none of the things that we've previously mentioned are possible in our own strength. If we try to apply them by gritting our teeth, making a fresh resolve and trying a bit harder, we will always fail. To apply and see working spiritual principles we need spiritual strength.

(A) *The Source Of Our Strength Is Jesus!*

The apostle John tells us, *"Ye are of God, little children, and have overcome them: because greater is he that is in you, than he that is in the world."* (1 John 4:4, AV). It is the revelation of the greatness of Christ within our lives which empowers us to live effectively, even at times of hardship. The Scriptures also say, *".... Christ in you, the hope of glory."* (Colossians 1:27). We will always have a strong confidence of the glory of God breaking through, even in the darkest moment of our lives, when we live by the revelation of the presence of Jesus within us.

In our society today, the storms of life are such that people turn to drink, drugs, the occult, false religions and even suicide, searching for a way out of their difficulties. Sadly, some Christians, because of the flood of their problems, turn away from God, the Church and from individual fellowship. The source of our strength though, especially in times of trouble is found in Matthew 8:25, *"And they went and woke him, saying, "Save, Lord; we are perishing."*

In the crisis the disciples turned to the Lord and they used the name of Jesus! That's the best thing we can do in any storm, because there is power in the name of Jesus! The Bible says, *"And it shall be that Whoever calls on the name of the Lord shall be saved."* (Acts 2:21). This is not only relevant for the initial salvation we receive when we first become Christians; It is also essential for the salvation we need in our daily lives, against everything that would seek to threaten our well being. The disciples, in the midst of the storm, knew that if they could make Jesus aware of their situation, then there was hope for them! It is in turning to the Lord that miracles happen!

This was very much the case for a foreign student I met recently, in her late twenties, who had come to live in this country. Though not a Christian, she decided to attend a meeting that I was speaking at in Essex. This woman was going through a personal storm in her life that she saw no way out of. Her marriage had broken up and she had also been harshly rejected by her own family. As I spoke that morning on, "The power of Christ to deliver," she responded, along with others and came forward saying that she wanted to become a Christian. We prayed together and she committed her life to Jesus. That morning she went home a changed person, and in turning to the Lord had found a strength beyond herself to overcome and stand for God.

When we are overwhelmed by the flood of our problems we need to focus on **CHRIST** and not upon the **CRISIS!** This is why the Bible says, *"Thou wilt keep him in perfect peace, whose mind is stayed on thee."* (Isaiah 26:3, AV). We are reminded also by the Psalmist, who certainly had his fair share of trouble, *"God is our refuge and strength, a very present help in trouble."* (Psalm 46:1). Notice this verse says,

"God *Is*,"- not God was, or will be, but God *Is*! The eternal, ever present one. In every situation of difficulty, the Lord is there to help and it is from the relationship we have with Him that we receive strength to press on through the storm. That's why Paul's instructions in Ephesians 6:10 are so important: *"Finally, be strong in the Lord and in the strength of his might."* If you are standing in the might of Almighty God, then there is nothing that can defeat you!

(B) *The Source Of Our Strength Is The Fullness Of The Holy Spirit*

We're reminded again of the words of the prophet, in Isaiah 59:19, *"When the enemy shall come in like a flood, the Spirit of the Lord shall lift up a standard against him."* (AV). The fullness of the Holy Spirit enables us to rise up with new confidence. His power strengthens us to stand against all that the enemy would try to use in attacking our lives. In view of this, it is essential that as we seek to live the Christian life, we move beyond receiving the Holy Spirit at our conversion, to being, *".... clothed with power from on high."* (Luke 24:49).

The difference this makes to an individual, especially in their stand against storms, is seen in the change this brought to the life of Peter. Before being baptised in the Holy Spirit he was so afraid of persecution, that he denied ever knowing Jesus. Having been filled with the power of God though, he was able to preach to thousands on the day of Pentecost, with no fear for his life whatsoever.

The new strength that the Holy Spirit gives, is even more clearly seen when you look at the disciples who, after Christ's death, stood uncompromisingly preaching the gospel. Their action resulted in them being arrested, thrown into prison and beaten. After being threatened further, they were released, but the Bible says, *"Then they left the presence of the council, rejoicing that they were counted worthy to suffer dishonour for the name."* (Acts 5:41). These were changed men, empowered by the Holy Spirit. There was a fire in their hearts that the storm of persecution could not put out. In fact they considered such suffering a privilege!

Since the fullness of the Holy Spirit is an indispensable source of our strength, we need to take great care that our lives are lived in righteousness. We cannot afford to sin! The moment we grieve the Holy Spirit through unconfessed sin, wrong attitudes, or actions, it weakens our spiritual strength to stand against temptations and to overcome trials. We then become an easy target for Satan.

(C) *The Source Of Our Strength Is A Living Faith*

In 1 John 5:4 we are told, *".... this is the victory that overcomes the world, our faith."* If faith is able to overcome "the world," it will most certainly strengthen our lives to overcome whatever might confront us in our local, personal circumstances. This faith is the conviction that God is "for us" and that we are not left alone in our situation to get by as best we can. It is the faith that even when the Lord appears to be *"asleep in the boat,"* unaware of what is going on; not doing anything about our crisis, we still believe that all will be well. Notice that in Matthew 8:26 Jesus expected them to have faith, even though their situation looked extremely serious and their circumstances severe. He says, *".... Why are you afraid, O men of little faith?"*

The only way to have a living faith is to feed it! Somebody once said, "Feed your faith and your doubts will starve to death!" This is why the scripture tells us, *"So then, faith cometh by hearing, and hearing by the word of God."* (Romans 10:17, AV). One of the best verses of scripture to build up faith, is a three fold promise found in one verse. It says, *"for the Lord your God is with you, to fight for you against your enemies, to give you the victory."* (Deuteronomy 20:4). If we only had this verse to hold on to in the midst of the storm, but were prepared to believe it, nothing could possibly defeat us! God has promised not only to be with us, but to fight for us, and he makes clear that not only will He fight for us, He will also give us the victory! Having this faith, we can truly say with conviction, - "The Battle Belongs To The Lord!"

We come now to the last aspect of the story we are considering and it is:

Thirdly, - THE SIGN OF HIS SOVEREIGNTY

(A) *The Authority Of His Word*

We read in the passage about the storm on the lake, *".... Then he rose and rebuked the winds and the sea...."* (verse 26). Just one word from the lips of Jesus is all it takes to deal with Satan and to still any storm.

When we think of the storm of sickness, the Centurion in the Bible recognised the Sovereign authority of Jesus when he said, *".... speak the word only, and my servant shall be healed."* (Matthew 8:8, AV). Looking at the storm of demonic bondage and oppression, we read, *"That evening they brought to him many who were possessed with demons; and he cast out the spirits with a word...."* (Matthew 8:16). Also, Jesus spoke to the storm of death, with all its darkness and finality, leaving people utterly helpless. He simply commanded life to come back into a dead body that had been in the grave four days. All He said was, *".... Lazarus, come out!"* (John 11:43) and the man came back to life again! Is it any wonder that people said of Jesus, *".... No man ever spoke like this man."* (John 7:46).

The authority and power of God's word changes situations, sometimes when we least expect it. While speaking at a mid-week Bible study in Kent I was under the impression that all those present were Christians. Because of this, the message was in no way evangelistic, but directed towards believers. Unknown to myself though, in the congregation was a man who was in the grip of the occult. He'd been dabbling in various areas of witchcraft and was bound by drugs. On top of this was the added confusion of his parents being Jehovah's Witnesses. After the meeting he asked for prayer saying he wanted to become a Christian and know Christ as his Saviour. That night the word of God challenged his heart and although the "gospel" as such wasn't preached, God had spoken directly to him and the young man recognised the authority of who he was listening to.

(B) *The Right Question To Ponder*

There are always many questions racing around in our minds when we're going through a crisis. So much that we don't understand, yet want answers to. The danger of reflecting on the wrong things is that it swiftly brings us to inaccurate conclusions. The wisest question to ponder though, is seen in verse 27; *"What sort of man is this, that even winds and sea obey him?"*

This simple question was asked by the disciples, after they had witnessed the power of Jesus over the raging storm and again it reveals the sign of His sovereignty. It opens our eyes to the revelation of who He is, bringing fresh hope and reassurance. Sometimes in the stress of life we can lose sight of Jesus and let things get all out of proportion. When we are going through any difficulty, we need to stop the racing thoughts and the whirlwind of our emotions and ask ourselves that same basic question. As we do so, the Holy Spirit brings to us the revelation of Jesus as Healer, Deliverer, Prince of Peace, Provider, Shepherd, Priest and King etc.; whatever is relevant to meet our need.

This question brings home to us the truth that Jesus is no ordinary man; He is the Lord! The sign of His sovereignty is that He is the Sovereign God in absolute control; Lord of every situation! The Bible gives us a wonderful picture of this truth when it says, *"The Lord sits enthroned over the flood; the Lord sits enthroned as King forever."* (Psalm 29:10). What a marvellous revelation of Jesus. Here we see

Him totally confident, in full control and with the storm underneath His feet!

As we ask ourselves, *"What sort of man is this?"* we are reminded also, that He is not just the Lord, but the Lord Jesus Christ. The word Christ in the Greek means, "The anointed one," and the Bible teaches us that there is an anointing which breaks the yoke of all oppression. Every struggle, disappointment, discouragement and sickness that would seek to restrict and trouble our lives, Jesus has been anointed to deal with. The scriptures say that, *"God anointed Jesus of Nazareth with the Holy Spirit and with power; he went about doing good and healing all who were oppressed by the devil for God was with him."* (Acts 10:38).

(C) *The Banner Of Victory*

Christ's sovereignty is revealed again in the words of Isaiah 59:19 that say, *".... When the enemy shall come in like a flood, the Spirit of the Lord shall lift up a standard against him."* This Standard is the distinctive flag, the ensign in battle. It's the banner to gather around and to fight under. It's the flag with the emblem of triumph on, declaring victory in every conflict! In the storm, the Spirit of God raises up in the face of Satan, who is the author of all trouble, that banner which proclaims the message of the blood of Jesus Christ.

This speaks to the enemy of, **Christ's Conquest At The Cross**. Here Jesus accomplished a final and irrevocable defeat over Satan. It was through the cross that every demonic plan and power of the evil one was defeated. The apostle was confident of this when he wrote regarding the victory of Jesus at the cross. Paul said, *"He disarmed the principalities and powers and made a public example of them, triumphing over them....."* (Colossians 2:15).

The Power of the blood declares, **Our Victory Over Satan**. This is why the Bible shows that even if our stand for Christ should cost us our lives, we shall still remain victorious. God's word says of those in the last days, going through great trials, *"And they have conquered him by the blood of the Lamb and by the word of their testimony, and they loved not their lives even unto death."* (Revelation 12:11).

Also, the power of the blood speaks of, **The Covenant Promises Of God's Word**. The Bible says, *"For all the promises of God find their yes in him."* (2 Corinthians 1:20). These promises are all the more made certain and sure because they have been sealed and ratified by the blood of Christ. We are in covenant relationship with God and He has bound Himself to His promises by that blood covenant!

The last part of verse 26 in our account of the storm is extremely meaningful; *"Then he rose and rebuked the winds and the sea; and there was a **great calm**."* This is God's will for us all, and it is the only way we can remain in victory, walking consistently. In the storms of our life He wants us to know that inner peace, and "great calm," whatever we may face.

Therefore, because storms are certain, we need to be "anchored" firmly in Christ; 100% committed to Him. We do not have to accept our situation in a defeatist way. Instead we can choose to be a victor rather than a victim. As we've already mentioned, in our own strength it's impossible, but we can turn to Jesus as Lord, and call upon Him as the Christ the anointed one. In doing so we will experience His provision to meet our every need and then, in reality, we shall stand firm as overcomers in the storms of life!

THIRD KEY
GRASPING GRACE

An amusing story is told of a family who were entertaining the local vicar and his wife for an evening meal. Due to the occasion, the hostess was very anxious to make a good impression and for their guests to see that they maintained Christian standards in their household. She decided therefore, to ask her five year old son to 'say grace' as they all gathered around the meal table together. At this suggestion the small lad looked a little blank and awkward, not really knowing quite what to say. His mother though, being quick to realise this, gave him a reassuring smile, followed swiftly by the words, *"Well darling, just say what daddy said this morning at breakfast."* Then, as only young children can, he tightly closed his eyes and dutifully repeated the words he'd heard only that morning, as he prayed, *"Oh God, we've got those awful people coming for dinner tonight!"*

While for many, "grace" is nothing more than something to be said with bowed heads at the meal table; its meaning has far greater implications, that should be life changing for us all. A right understanding of this is essential for consistent Christian living. This is because grace is so much more than a **DOCTRINE**; - it is a **DYNAMIC POWER!** Building our lives upon the revelation of this truth is probably the one thing beyond anything else that enables us to continue standing for God.

There are many things that could be said about this word to help explain its significance, for example, grace is:

(A) *The Triumph Of God's Goodness Over Man's Evil!*

As we look at the decline of standards in society today and how lawlessness has increased, we could well hold our hands up in horror at what is happening in our nation. In spite of this though, the Bible says, *"But where sin abounded, grace did much more abound."* (Romans 5: 20, AV). It is reassuring to know that while the influence and effect of sin may be great, praise God the power of grace is greater! In practical terms this means, there is no **Person**, no **Place** and no **Predicament** beyond the grace of God.

(B) *The Expression Of God's Love*

Grace is the gift of God and is an expression of His willingness to meet our needs. We are able to experience this, not because of any merit of our own or any virtue in our character; it is the undeserved kindness of God choosing to touch our lives, - often when we least expect it and always when we most need it. For example, when problems strike and we're confronted by a crisis, or at times when we anxiously wonder how we are going to get through a particular situation. It's then that grace comes in to uphold and sustain us.

(C) *The Practical Evidence That 'God Is For Us'*

Sometimes we do need practical, concrete evidence, because just a scripture being quoted by someone, or simply the reminder of a doctrinal statement, seems at times insufficient. There needs occasionally to be some supernatural expression of God's miraculous power and love. The very heart of the gospel is the good news that not only are we 'saved' by grace, but we are kept and sustained by grace as well. John Newton, the slave trader who was converted to Christ, put it so well when writing from his own experience. He penned the words, *"Through many dangers, toils and snares, I have already come, 'tis grace that brought me safe thus far and grace will lead me home."* Simply seeing grace as a doctrine is inadequate to keep us living consistently for God, but when we have the revelation that it is a dynamic, mighty power, impacting our lives, this has a transforming effect.

As we consider in greater depth this truth, let us look at three major areas where the importance of grace is revealed from 2 Corinthians 8:9. Here we read, *"For you know the grace of our Lord Jesus Christ, that though he was rich, yet for your sake he became poor, so that by his poverty you might become rich."*

Firstly, - THE PERSONAL DISCOVERY OF GRACE

God's word says, *"For you know the grace...."* We can only ever move from doctrine to dynamic power and experience the effect of grace, when we have a personal discovery. It needs to drop from our head to our hearts and become reality in our life. The vital thing is for us to 'know,' not just intellectually, theoretically, or even theologically, but from personal experience. Jesus illustrated the power that is invested and imparted in this word, 'to know' when He said, *".... and you will know the truth, and the truth will make you free."* (John 8:32).

This personal discovery of grace begins with 'knowing' Christ as our saviour, but continues as we look to Him as the source of our total supply. One of the main reasons why so many Christians fail to live a consistent life is because they make the mistake of looking to themselves when things get difficult. We need to learn the importance of looking to Jesus rather than battling on in our own strength and understanding. The Bible says, *"The Word became flesh and dwelt among us, full of grace and truth...."* (John 1:14). Then again in verse 16, *".... of his grace have we all received, grace upon grace."* There is an abundance of grace to be found in Jesus. We don't have to look anywhere else!

The difference that 'knowing' the dynamic power of grace makes is seen in the way it brings the following things into reality in our experience:

(A) *Assurance That Our Life Is Important To God*

Many people today struggle with the problem of a poor self image. Their low sense of worth seems to undermine all that they try to do.

If we feel insignificant and of little importance or value, how can we believe God is going to answer our prayers, use our life, or respond to us in times of need. The personal discovery of grace though, reminds us that among the millions of the world, "God loves me and has chosen to bless and use my life!" The excitement this revelation brings is expressed so well in the life of Mary. When she made this personal discovery herself she could not contain her joy as she cried out, *".... My soul magnifies the Lord, and my spirit rejoices in God my Saviour,...... for he who is mighty has done great things for me......"* (Luke 1:46-49).

We are not merely a little speck in this great expanse of a universe. The personal discovery of grace reassures us that God has a plan and purpose for our life, which is not limited by our qualifications or credentials. An ordinary life can be made extraordinary by the grace of God! We read in the scriptures that grace deliberately chooses the most unlikely people. It says, *"God chose what is foolish in the world to shame the wise, God chose what is weak in the world to shame the strong, God chose what is low and despised in the world, even the things that are not, to bring to nothing things that are."* (1 Corinthians 1:27&28).

(B) *The Breath Of Life Into Religion*

I have to smile at the story told of a young man who invited his close, non-Christian friend to church one Sunday. The newcomer was greeted at the door by a dark-suited man who vigorously pumped his hand and inquired in a tone of absolute seriousness, "Have you found the Lord?" "No," the visitor replied somewhat nervously, "Have you lost Him?" Religion without the dynamic power of grace is dead and dull and of little interest to the unconverted. It is often this absence of grace in people's experience that causes them to find it difficult to relate to those without Christ. In their striving to do what they think they 'ought to,' they become awkward and insensitive.

The absence of grace is also the cause of so much dogmatism and harshness in peoples attitudes towards others. External rules and regulations can never make us acceptable to God and certainly never make us attractive to the unconverted. Knowing the truth of grace though, has got great power to set us free from the legalism of petty concerns and critical suspicions. It delivers us from sterile Christianity, devoid of joy and dominated by the fear of failure. It releases us from the religious bondage of striving to please God out of a slavish sense of duty. As a result, the personal discovery of grace enables us to enter into a spiritual rest where we can be natural and secure in the unconditional love of God.

Many Christians today find themselves trying to justify their existence, impress others or gain acceptance from God in their work, ministry or their position in the Church. We don't have to strive to gain God's approval or struggle to attain the acceptance of His love, nor anyone else's. We can rest in the revelation that grace means, God loves us not because of our performance, but simply because of who we are; His precious children.

(C) *Confidence In God's Forgiveness Regardless Of Our Past*

Two of the saddest words in the English language are, 'If only.' How often we find ourselves thinking, "If only I hadn't said what I did to that person," or, "If only I'd taken a different course of action." We have all got things in our past we'd sooner not be reminded of; incidents that we'd rather forget. Perhaps things we've said, done, or haven't done. Whilst this is true, we cannot live our lives consistently for God as we dwell on past regrets.

If the apostle Paul had lived with the, 'If only' mentality, he would never have achieved the tremendous things he did. His life before being converted was that of a murderer, blasphemer and a persecutor of the Christian faith. The regrets of Paul's past could have been like a 'ball and chain' around him, and would have been an immense hindrance. It was knowing the grace of God's forgiveness, that enabled Paul to say, *".... one thing I do, forgetting what lies behind and straining forward to what lies ahead...."* (Philippians 3:13). This personal 'knowing' enables us to come out from under the yoke of slavery to the past, so that we can enjoy the rights and privileges of what it means to be free!

This is just what happened to a man at a church I was speaking at in Colchester one Sunday morning. He had been a backsliden Christian for fifteen years and had a great many regrets about some of the things he'd done in that time. He was going through a period of deep depression and in all those years had not been anywhere near a church. That morning though, for some reason he couldn't explain, he just woke up and decided to go along to the service.

As he sat listening, the Lord not only convicted him of his former life, but also gave him confidence that he could be restored and forgiven. This man came forward in repentance at the end of the meeting and as he recommitted his life to God found a joy and peace that was obvious for all to see! This unmerited favour of forgiveness and release from the guilt of our past is made clear in the words of the Psalmist who could say, *"If thou O Lord, should mark iniquities, Lord who could stand? But there is forgiveness with thee...."* (Psalm 130:3&4).

(D) *New Motivation In Service For God*

This is so important if we are wanting our lives to make a positive impression on others. As we serve the Lord it needs to be with a gladness and enthusiasm that is clear to those around us. Some Christians however, show such little excitement and enthusiasm about their faith that what they present to a sad and depressed generation is only more of the same, but in religious clothing!

New motivation changes our outlook on life to live 100% for God. I remember praying with a man in his mid seventies, from Longbridge,

Birmingham, for whom this was true. The power of the Holy Spirit had fallen upon him and he was flat out on the floor. When eventually he stood up, he came to me with great excitement saying, "Yan, I've given myself to God this morning, body, soul and spirit!" Another example that comes to mind is that of an eighty year old lady from Stoke who after the meeting asked for prayer. God had touched her in a wonderful way and she said, "I'll be going on holiday to Spain for several weeks soon and I'm going to take some gospel booklets and spend my whole time witnessing to the British tourists!"

Doctrine alone cannot accomplish this sort of motivation, but the dynamic, miraculous power of God's grace is able to put a new fire within us. This will not only stir us into action, but keep us active, especially through hard and difficult times, when normally we would perhaps be tempted to give up. The very power that enabled Paul to remain consistent in the face of great opposition and incredible pressure was this grace. He could say, *"For I am the least of the apostles, unfit to be called an apostle, because I persecuted the Church of God. But by the grace of God I am what I am, and his grace toward me was not in vain. On the contrary, I worked harder than any of them, though it was not I, but the grace of God which is within me."* (1 Corinthians 15:9&10).

The next aspect about the power of grace from 2 Corinthians 8:9 that keeps us living consistently for God is:

Secondly, - THE PRICE OF GRACE

When we think of this, what we are talking about is the cost to Jesus of our salvation. The revelation of His great love for us is the very thing that draws our hearts in glad service for Him. Paul could say, *"We love him, because he first loved us."* (1 John 4:19, AV).

The hymn writer, when thinking about the price of grace as he considered the cross, had to conclude with the words, *"love so amazing, so divine, demands my life, my soul, my all."* It was because of the cross that our hardened hearts first began to melt and it is there we need to return when that devotion begins to wane. In looking then at the price of grace Paul says, *".... though he was rich, yet for your sake he became poor...."* (2 Corinthians 8:9). We need to see ourselves in that verse and be able to put our name in that scripture. For me Jesus became so poor! It is reminding ourselves of the extent of that poverty that makes such an impact upon our lives.

This was very much the case for a young man by the name of Charles T. Studd. He was born into a wealthy British family in 1862. As he grew up and went to Cambridge University he became an outstanding cricket player. In his third year at the University, he was converted to Christ while attending a Moody-Sankey meeting. Although the whole world seemed to be at his feet he announced he was giving away his personal fortune, leaving his cricketing career and becoming a missionary in China. For nine years he served with Hudson Taylor's Mission until poor health forced him to return to England in 1894.

A few years later, a growing burden led him to begin plans to evangelise Africa, from the Nile to the Niger. In 1910 he left for the continent and in 1919 he established the 'World-wide Evangelisation Crusade.' C.T. Studd explained in just one sentence what it was that had kept him going through much hardship and many discouraging times when he said, "If Jesus Christ be God and died for me, then no sacrifice that I can make, can be too great for Him."

In Philippians 2:6-8 we find described something of the extent of the price of grace, and the poverty that Jesus experienced. It says, *"Let this mind be in you, which was also in Christ Jesus: Who, being in the form of God, thought it not robbery to be equal with God: But made himself of no reputation, and took on him the form of a servant, and was made in the likeness of men: And being found in fashion as a man, he humbled himself, and became obedient unto death, even the death of the cross.* " (AV). Why do you suppose the Bible emphasises, *'even the death of the cross?'* Simply because crucifixion was one the most humiliating and horrifying ways that a person could die in those times. This form of death was always kept for the dregs of society and the lowest of the low, yet Jesus subjected Himself to such suffering for us.

One of the best explanations to help our understanding of this word grace is found in that old acrostic, G.R.A.C.E. - **G**reat **R**iches **A**t **C**hrist's **E**xpense. - The expense to Jesus of His innocence, His security, His dignity and His relationship with God was all laid on the line, as He "emptied Himself."

While for us grace comes as a free gift, the cost to Jesus was immense. The person who at one time filled the entire universe, restricted Himself as a tiny seed to be confined in the womb of Mary. The one who for eternity past had been worshipped, honoured, exalted and adored by the angels of heaven, stepped down to be born in a dirty stable and regarded as illegitimate in eyes of others. He was rejected, humiliated, abused and put on a cross. Then, such was the poverty of His grace, He was laid in a borrowed grave. Christ the King became so poor that He didn't even have his own burial place! Furthermore, Jesus, who never for a single moment had ever been separated from the presence of His father, even while here on earth, finds Himself forsaken by God, as he cries out in torment on the cross, *"…. My God, My God, why hast thou forsaken me?"* (Mark 15:34). - Why? It was for our sake Jesus became so poor!

Jesus knew only too well how short our memories are and that what, at one time, made a deep impression upon us, can all too quickly be forgotten in its impact on our lives. It was because of this that just before He died, Jesus instituted what we now call, "The Lord's Supper," "Communion," or "The Breaking of Bread," and He said, *"…. Do this in remembrance of me."* (Luke 22:19). Notice how Jesus took two of the most common, ordinary things of life in those days to represent His suffering. Just bread and simply wine. There was no great pomp and ceremony, because Jesus didn't want us to ever get away from the poverty of Grace.

The final aspect of grace to consider and one that again shows us its dynamic power enabling us to live consistently is:

Thirdly, - THE PURPOSE OF GRACE

Having been reconciled to God we should be living in the fullness of Christ's blessings. This is why Paul now explains God's intention of grace, from 2 Corinthians 8:9. He says, *".... so that by his poverty you might become rich."* Jesus came not only to RESCUE our lives from the power of sin; not just to RELEASE us from the power of Satan. He came also to RESTORE back to us all that had been stolen by the evil one, since the time when man first walked together with God in the garden of Eden. We see therefore, that the purpose of grace is three fold. It helps us live in the blessing of:

(A) *Abundance Rather Than Poverty*

Too many Christians live as 'paupers' spiritually when they should be living like Kings! In spite of the fact that we sin, make many mistakes and are far from perfect, grace has enriched our lives in every possible way. This is demonstrated as Paul writes to the church at Corinth. He was aware of the immorality, idolatry, party spirit and division that was going on in the church and he was going to address those issues. The first thing he says though, in full knowledge of their unrighteousness is, *"I give thanks to God always for you because of the grace of God which was given you in Christ Jesus, that in every way you were enriched in him, with all speech and all knowledge - even as the testimony to Christ was confirmed among you so that you are not lacking in any spiritual gift...."* (1 Corinthians 1:4-7).

God's grace provides for all our needs, spiritually, physically, emotionally and materially. This is why Paul could say to the church at

Philippi, even while he himself was in a prison cell, *"My God will supply every need of yours according to his riches in glory in Christ Jesus."* (Philippians 4:19).

In view of how much Jesus was prepared to suffer and the extent to which He was willing to be made poor for us, should we not be appropriating all that has been provided through the cross and promised in the scriptures? To make clear how rich and full that provision is and how abundant His grace should be in our lives Paul says, *"God is able to make all grace abound to you, so that in all things at all times, having all that you need, you will abound in every good work."* (2 Corinthians 9:8, NIV).

(B) *Godliness Rather Than Compromise*

We are responsible to live pure and holy lives; to be distinctive and different in our values and standards from those who are without Christ. This is why Paul writes to the Romans saying, *"Do you not know that God's kindness,* (which is God's grace) *is meant to lead you to repentance?"* (Romans 2:4). God is so good that He doesn't want us to live in compromise, nor have double standards. Part of the working of His grace is to convict us when there are areas of unrighteousness in our life, so that we will be brought to repentance and want to change.

In writing to the Corinthians Paul says, *"We entreat you not to accept the grace of God in vain."* (2 Corinthians 6:1). We can experience God's goodness in salvation and know His power to change our lives, then find ourselves doing and saying things that are no different from those who are without Christ. One reason for this is a misunderstanding of grace, where our new liberty leads us into license. We say, "I'm no longer **under law**, I'm **under grace**, so I don't have to be legalistic and rigid about the discipline of reading the scriptures, praying or evangelising etc. I no longer have to bother about what people think, because I've been freed from all that!" This 'pendulum swing' and distorted view of grace takes us to an extreme where we neglect the discipline of righteousness and find ourselves compromising God's standard of holiness.

I experienced an example of this, while on holiday with my family in America some years ago. Just a few miles from where we were staying was a well know entertainer, who was star billing at a particular club. I knew he was a born again Christian and so I went along to see if I could meet him. Having spoken to the manager of the club and mentioned that I was a minister from England, I asked if I could see this person. Eventually we got together and it was a joy and privilege to be with him. He was enthusiastic about his love for Christ and clearly a genuine Christian.

After spending some time with him, I then sat down to watch his act. Sadly this turned out to be a great disappointment. Throughout his performance it was full of sexual innuendoes and smutty jokes. Even swear words were used quite frequently. As I looked on I thought to myself, "the grace of God in vain." This incident I only mention by way of illustration. It isn't for us to point the finger at others and criticise their standards, but we can learn from their mistakes. We need to look within our own hearts and make sure that our lives are not a contradiction of what we claim to believe.

In fairness to the person I'm speaking about, I wrote to him afterwards expressing my concern and also talked with him on the phone. In our conversation he acknowledged that the things in his act were wrong and he stated that they were now no longer any part of his performance. All I could say having heard this was, "Thank you Lord for your grace that leads to repentance!"

We need to see, as Christians, that grace makes no less demands on us than the law made. It sets up for us the standard of Christ and says, "This is what grace expects." We are no less obligated to holiness and obedience because we are 'under grace,' than if we'd been 'under the law.' This is not legalism, it is love, and is why Jesus said, *"If you love me, you will keep my commandments."* (John 14:15).

To make clear the truth that God's grace trains us to live in the blessing of godliness and not compromise we read in Titus 2:11-14, *"For the grace of God has appeared for the salvation of all men, training us to renounce irreligion and worldly passions, and to live sober, upright and godly lives in this present world, awaiting our blessed hope, the appearing of the glory of our great God and Saviour Jesus Christ, who gave himself for us to redeem us from all iniquity and to purify for himself, a people of his own, who are zealous for good deeds."*

(C) *Victory Rather Than Defeat*

As we have emphasised in the previous chapters, maintaining victory and living consistently is the normal Christian life! God wants us to know how to be victorious in life's problems, whatever they might be. One of the main reasons why few manage to live the life that the Bible promises is possible, is because they have failed to see this wonderful revelation of grace. When Christians see beyond the doctrine and experience its dynamic miraculous power, then it truly is life changing!

The apostle Paul was a man who seemed to be able to rise above every situation that tried to defeat him. Although he encountered much hardship and many set backs, he maintained a victorious, consistent life, because he understood this principle of grace. It was the revelation of this that made him what he was. Paul could say, *"If, because of one man's trespass, death reigned through that one man, much more will those who receive the abundance of grace and the free gift of righteousness reign in life through the one man Jesus Christ."* (Romans 5:12). Notice that the scripture says, ***"reign in life;"***- Not in the great "bye and bye" when we die and get to heaven, but in the here and now of every day experience. Paul was an overcomer, not in his own ability and determination, but through the "abundance of grace" that he lived in.

To see this truth at work in the lives of ordinary people who were put under the immense pressure of threats, beatings, imprisonment and even death, we only need to look at the first Christians. The power of grace brought them the strength to live vibrant, victorious lives, even though they faced intense persecution and severe opposition. The Bible says, *"And with great power the apostles gave their testimony to the resurrection of the Lord Jesus, and great grace was upon them all."* (Acts 4:33).

HOW WE RECEIVE

There are two simple ways that each of us can be sure of experiencing this same grace. **Firstly,** we must receive God's grace *Humbly.* This means we swallow our pride and admit our need. We must renounce our independence and disregard our embarrassment. This first step of honesty and reality is essential. The Bible says, *".... God opposes the proud, but gives grace to the humble. Humble yourselves therefore under the mighty hand of God, that in due time he may exalt you."* (1 Peter 5:5&6).

An example of someone I met, who wasn't prepared to do this, was a man who came for prayer after a meeting that I was speaking at in Colchester. He began by saying, "God has called me into full time service. I've just finished an immoral relationship and I'm not going to any regular church, because I believe in just "moving around" churches, but I do feel called to evangelise." When I suggested that before we prayed, we needed to talk about his submission to the leadership of a local church and the need for commitment and accountability, his eyes immediately began to flash with anger. He snarled at me and got very nasty, saying, "I don't want to hear anything like that, I just want you to pray for God's blessing on my life!" There was clearly no sign of wanting to humble himself and certainly no way that I felt able to pray for what he initially requested.

Secondly, we receive God's grace *Confidently*. Without fear, or doubting that God will answer our prayer. We must come before God expecting Him to honour His word. The instruction God gives is, *"Let us then with confidence draw near to the throne of grace, that we may receive mercy and find grace to help in time of need."* (Hebrews 4:16).

I remember a seventy five year old man who expressed this confidence. He was in a meeting that I was speaking at in Devon. This person was in great pain, suffering with gout in both wrist joints and had experienced restricted movement for four years. That night I was talking about the healing power of Christ and before I got round to giving an invitation for people to respond, he had stood up and made his way down to the front waiting for prayer. As we prayed God's power came upon him and he fell to the floor. When he got up again, he was so excited that he turned round to the rest of the congregation and testified that the pain was totally gone and his wrists were healed and free from restriction!

The dynamic power of God's grace bringing healing, forgiveness, encouragement, renewal, restoration and motivation is therefore available to us all. The price has been paid in full by Jesus; it was for our sakes that He became so poor. Right now today, the Lord wants us to be living in the blessing of abundance and not poverty; godliness rather than compromise; and victory instead of defeat!

✦ FOURTH KEY ✦
CHRIST CENTRED CONSECRATION

It's not so much what we say, but how we live that causes people to sit up and take notice. This truth is underlined in a humorous story I heard recently, of a young curate who was desperate to grip the attention of his sleepy church members. One Sunday, half way through his message, he abruptly interrupted the sermon with the words, "I remember the time when I was in the arms of another mans wife!" Instantly, everyone's eyebrows were raised, as they sat listening with bated breath for the revelations that were to follow. The curate then added, "She was the wife of my father!"- much to the amusement of his congregation.

Not long afterward the Bishop got to hear of this incident and decided that the joke would make an impressive introduction to his next sermon. When this opportunity came, he stood up in the great Cathedral before a vast congregation, including the Lord Mayor, town councillors and civic dignitaries. Then with great confidence he began, "I remember the time I was in the arms of another mans wife!" A deathly hush suddenly descended upon the place, then after a long pause the Bishop stammered nervously, fumbling through his notes, and eventually said, ".... Just for the moment I can't remember whose wife she was!"

I am so grateful to God, that He is not calling us to be "stand up comedians!" Instead, He is changing people's lives to reflect His glory." We can all make a powerful impact on others and never more so than when we are living consistently for the Lord. We don't have to rely on impressive oratory, sensational gimmicks, or clever ideas, but simply let the reality of Christ be seen in us. One of the most challenging, life changing concepts in the whole of the Bible that enables us to do this is, Christ Centred Consecration.

One definition of the word consecration is; **"To be set apart as sacred and dedicated to God."** We need to see our lives in these terms and be confident that this is a good description of ourselves. It doesn't mean that we have to become like nuns or monks, closeted away in a monastery somewhere; quite the reverse. It means that we are distinctive disciples of Jesus, making a difference in our community, as we reflect the very character of God.

The clearest example of this, and the surest way to remain consistent, can be summed up in one verse expressed by the apostle Paul. He could say, *"I have been crucified with Christ; it is no longer I who live but Christ who lives in me; and the life I now live in the flesh I live by faith in the Son of God, who loved me and gave himself for me."* (Galatians 2:20). These words describe well the life of the apostle and reveal the secret of his steadfastness in service. This declaration was more than words though; it was a life style that involved a **discipline of the mind**, an **attitude of the heart**, and a **resolve of the will**, to live for the glory of God!

A lady that I met from a church at Westcliffe on Sea, in Essex was a good example of this. She came after the close of the meeting and said, "You were preaching here five months ago. When I came into the service that evening I wasn't a Christian, but just one sentence from your message convicted me and that night I committed my life to Christ!" She then went on to say, "Since that time I've been baptised in water, baptised in the Holy Spirit and I've led four people to Jesus!" It was clear on her face and in the excitement of her voice that she intended her life to make a difference to others.

As we look at Galatians 2:20, let us consider three components of this verse that enables Jesus to be more clearly seen in our lives and causes us to live a more effective life for the Lord.

Firstly, - DEATH TO SELF

Paul could say with absolute conviction, *"I have been crucified with Christ...."* This is where we must begin if our life is to know any significant change. We live in a society today that is obsessed with self-gratification, self-promotion, self-preservation, self-awareness, self-assertiveness and self-interest. However, as far as you and I are concerned, as Christians, all that centres on 'I', 'Me' and 'My' must die. It needs to be put to death and accounted as dead! This change of thinking alone would deal with well over 95% of all counselling problems and the clamour for ministry today. I certainly believe in the need for counselling and ministry. Spending time with those who have problems and bringing deliverance and healing into peoples lives is important. There is such a pre-occupation today though, in the Church, as in the world, with, "My needs," "My problems," and "My fulfilment," that everything has become focused on self.

The danger of this pre-occupation is very serious, because self-centredness is the cause of emptiness in religion and in relationships. It brings a coldness into marriage, friction into families, unrest into society and impotence into the Church! We are robbed of God's blessing and power as we turn inward, concerned primarily with ourselves. To avoid this danger we must live with the revelation and sincerity expressed by Paul. This certainly doesn't deny the importance of our problems, nor does it over simplify the complexity of some of the issues we are confronted by. What it does do though, which is so vital, is that it presents an answer to those situations we would not normally consider. The reality is that the **Altar** is where we are going to be **Altered**, and nowhere else!

We can see how death to self is the answer to so many of the issues that try to weaken our life, and which cause us to be inconsistent, in the following ways:

(A) *Security In Times Of Trouble*

Although the problems of life are inescapable, when we have died to ourselves, we see things not just from our own perspective and how it affects us, we start to view things from God's perspective. It's at this point that we begin to discover the troubles of life can be the means of strengthening and shaping our character. The words of James then take on a new understanding as we read, *"Count it all joy my brethren, when you meet various trials, for you know that the testing of your faith produces steadfastness. And let steadfastness have it's full effect, that you may be perfect and complete, lacking nothing."* (James 1:2-4).

If we are honest, when we are faced with a crisis, or are going through painful circumstances, it is totally impossible to, *"Count it all joy,"*- unless we have first died to ourselves. If however, we have done so, we start to see that something good and positive can come out of even what appears to be the most, confusing, dark and negative of circumstances.

The illustration of photography is helpful here because we are reminded that in every negative, there is a latent image needing to be developed. When you first look at the negative, it appears dark and puzzling, not making very much sense, but you don't throw it away. You develop the negative in the dark room and not the light. It is the same with our problems. In the dark and confusing times of our life God is able to bring a positive out of every negative, when we are willing to die to ourselves. Paul lived by this belief, in all the trials he went through and therefore could say, *"... we were so utterly, unbearably crushed that we despaired of life itself. Why we felt that we had received the sentence of death; **but** that was to make us rely not on **ourselves** but on God who raises the dead."* (2 Corinthians 1:8&9). Paul believed that regardless of the troubles overshadowing him, something positive and good would eventually emerge.

(B) *Striving Against Temptation*

The temptation to satisfy "self" is a very real problem for every person. If anything can try to stop you living steadfastly for God then this can. Yielding to our sinful habits, desires and thought life, leaves us with a feeling of failure and condemnation. God's word explains that within us there is a constant battle going on, a tension that exists often daily. It says, *"For the desires of the flesh* (which is the self life) *are against the Spirit, and the desires of the Spirit are against the flesh; for these are opposed to each other, to prevent you from doing what you would."* (Galatians 5:17).

While this is true, the Bible teaches us that we are not left in a helpless state of frustration. It says, *"For sin will have no dominion over you...."* (Romans 6:14). God never guarantees anything that we cannot live in the good of. The big question is though, how do we manage to appropriate that sort of promise? We can only do so when we have first died to ourselves. This is what we find in scripture when Paul explains, *"For he who has died is freed from sin."* (Romans 6:7). A dead person cannot sin! There is no dead body that ever has any problem with lustful thoughts, wrong attitudes or thoughtless actions. Therefore Paul uses this strange image and develops this thought when he says, *"So you also must consider yourselves dead to sin and alive to God in Christ Jesus."* (Romans 6:11). This reckoning needs to take place in the battleground of our mind, it is here the battle is either won or lost. As we reckon in our minds, "I've died to that way of reacting and speaking." "I've died to that way of thinking; it's part of my old way of living,"- then we are able to walk in "newness of life!"

(C) *Struggling In Relationships*

The network of relationships can at times be like a minefield, where the explosion of anger and harsh words suddenly throws everything into chaos. This is so, whether we are talking about single people, or between husbands and wives. In relationships at work, within the family, or with our neighbours; this whole area is fraught with possible tension and stress.

There can be conflict and misunderstanding; circumstances when we feel we want to justify ourselves or stand up for our "rights!"

Certain incidents may cause us to over-react, or insist on our own way and as a result resentment and bitterness creep in. Also, there can be occasions when we feel unappreciated, unfulfilled and taken for granted, or we want to be recognised and accepted. When things don't go exactly as we want them to, or we feel hurt and offended, we can begin to retaliate in ways that only aggravate the situation. Conversely, another way we react is just not to bother and become indifferent towards the relationship.

In all of these situations, it is the self life that produces an unrighteous response and the only way to handle this is to be willing to die to ourselves. The teaching in scripture is, *"Do nothing out of selfish ambition or vain conceit, but in humility consider others better than yourselves. Each of you should look not only to your own interests but also to the interests of others. Your attitude should be the same as that of Christ Jesus."* (Philippians 2:3-5, NIV). The attitude of Christ was always to put other people's needs before His own. It was to give His life and not to expect to receive. Jesus was prepared to make the first move and reach out even when knowing He would be abused, rejected, let down, betrayed and taken for granted. With this attitude and intention behind all our actions tremendous release and restoration is brought into every aspect of relationships, especially the difficult ones that seem impossible and beyond hope.

(D) *Strength To Be Obedient*

God requires of us total obedience to His every word. The problem today is certainly not the teaching we receive, because we can listen to the best audio messages, watch the finest videos, read the most challenging books and attend the most anointed meetings. It isn't the clarity or quality of instruction that is the difficulty, but putting into practice what we know to be right, that's the problem!

Frequently our strength to be obedient is weakened because of our own plans, desires for success, personal preferences and our own comfort. Also, our concern about the cost to ourselves can hold us back and get in the way of doing God's will. Jesus faced this same challenge in the garden of Gethsemane. When He thought about the horror of the cross and the cost to Himself of doing God's will He said, *".... My Father, if it be possible, let this cup pass from me; nevertheless, not as I will,* (not what self wants) *but as thou wilt."* (Matthew 26:39). The triumph of Jesus over Satan was established not merely at the cross but there in the garden. It was when Jesus died to Himself that the victory was settled. This is the only way we can do God's will, particularly when it is something hard and costly to ourselves.

(E) *Safety From Deception*

The problem of deception is very common and especially in these days, as we are living in the "end times." God's word warns us that deception in the last days will be widespread and false prophets will be increasing. At the root of the majority of deception is the self life which is not surrendered. We hear of many going around today saying, "The Lord has told me...."or, "God has given me a word for you." Well praise God for revelation! I'm grateful for every prophetic utterance and believe we should be hearing more "Words of Knowledge." This is fine and needs to be encouraged, when the individual's life is submitted, accountable and teachable. However, a proud, independent, unteachable spirit can bring havoc into the Church and also to the lives of individuals. This is why Paul taught the importance of, *"Submitting yourselves one to another in the fear of God."* (Ephesians 5:21, AV).

We must all be in a place where we're under authority and accountable in our lives. It is essential that we have a humble attitude and are listening to one another; maintaining a teachable spirit, so that we can be corrected in love where necessary. Anyone who is unteachable, unaccountable, and unwilling to submit, is wide open to the deceptive powers of Satan and will not only be led out of God's will themselves, but they will lead others astray as well.

(F) *Supernatural Power To Witness*

The power of Christ's supernatural ability has been promised to all who will believe. Jesus said, *"Truly, truly, I say to you, he who believes in me will also do the works that I do; and greater works than these will he do, because I go to the father."* (John 14:12). Why is it, therefore, that people see such a minimal effect of that ability in their lives and the Church at large is not living in the good of this clear promise? It is because the self life robs us of such power and restricts our great potential. This can be seen in two extremes, both of which are firmly centred on self. The first is fear and is expressed in self consciousness where we start to say, "I can't do it, I'm not qualified." "What if I fail?" "What if I make a fool of myself, or I'm rejected?" Notice how all this fear and insecurity revolves around the "**I**," "**Me**" and "**My**" and will always be a hindrance to us.

The other way we are robbed of God's power and restricted, is over confidence in our own ability and strength. We need to recognise that relying on our plans, ideas and organisational skills must die, so that our boldness and ability is dependant upon God. Striving in the energy of the flesh has got to give way to confidence in the anointing of the Holy Ghost! This is why God's word says, *".... Not by might, nor by power, but by my Spirit says the Lord of hosts."* (Zechariah 4:6).

Secondly,- DEDICATION TO CHRIST

For every Christian, the positive aspect of death, is the resurrection that follows. The grave becomes the cradle of something new! New life is born out of that willingness to die and not until the principle of death has been established, will the experience of a resurrection life become a reality. This is why Paul, having begun by saying, *"I have been crucified with Christ,"* then goes on to say, *".... It is no longer I who live but Christ who lives in me."* The whole focus of thinking has now shifted away from self, to Christ. John the Baptist expressed the importance of this in his own life when he said, *"He must increase, but I must decrease."* (John 3:30). The point is transparent; as we are willing to get out of the way, the more clearly Jesus is seen and able to work through our lives.

As we previously mentioned, the Greek meaning of the word "Christ" is the "anointed one". What Paul was actually saying in Galatians 2:20 was, *"It is no longer myself who is living, but **the anointed one** that is living through me."* This is the Christ who said, *"The Spirit of the Lord is upon me, because he has anointed me to preach good news to the poor. He has sent me to proclaim release to the captives and recovering of sight to the blind, to set at liberty those who are oppressed, to proclaim the acceptable year of the Lord."* (Luke 4:18&19).

We will have no difficulty sharing the gospel; bringing freedom to those who are captive and no problem ministering healing to the broken hearted, when we grasp the revelation that it is not ourselves doing this, but the "anointed one" working through us! It is then that the life of Christ just flows naturally out from us. There is no striving, or reason to feel inadequate in situations of need. We simply find, as the scriptures say of those who believe, *".... Out of his heart shall flow rivers of living water."* (John 7:38).

A Living Sacrifice

Dedication to live firstly for the Lord rather than ourselves is such a major key in unlocking the reality of what we've spoken about so far. Many Christians though, fail to live in the experience of this because their lives operate on a completely wrong basis. It should not be a question of what we can get, how we can be blessed, or what we can receive. Rather our thinking should reflect the priority that is called for in Romans 12:1 *"I appeal to you therefore brethren, by the mercies of God, to present your bodies as a living sacrifice, holy and acceptable to God which is your spiritual worship."*

A "living sacrifice" requires a daily commitment! If we woke up every morning and began the day with this attitude, we would without doubt make an impact everywhere we went. Our daily lives then would not only meet the challenge of Jesus to follow Him, but would also encourage others, by our example, to live their lives dedicated to Christ. The degree of this dedication in following Christ is expressed in the words of Jesus when He says, *".... If any man would come after me, let him deny himself and take up his cross and follow me."* (Mark 8:34).

Dedication Expressed Through Discipleship

The radical nature of discipleship is fundamental to fruitful and effective service. It's interesting that Satan understands better than we do the importance of this principle; so much so that he has taken a legitimate biblical word and effectively eliminated it from the vocabulary of Christians today. As a result of abuse in the past through the "Heavy Shepherding Movement," submission and authority were taken to an extreme. Many people were damaged and you now rarely hear discipleship preached about and certainly not found in the conversation of Christians.

However, we have all been called in God's word not only to be disciples of Christ, but to make disciples of others. The only concept that New Testament believers had of being a Christian and following Jesus was discipleship. For this privilege they were prepared to give up everything! One of the best descriptions that I've ever heard of this commitment was written by the well known American author and Bible teacher, Dr Edwin Cole. He sums up what a disciple is in these terms:-

> "I am a disciple of Jesus Christ and am part of the fellowship of the unashamed. I have Holy Spirit power. The die has been cast. I've stepped over the line. The love of God controls me. The decision has been made. I am a disciple of His. I won't look back, let up, slow down or back away. My

past is redeemed. My present makes sense. My future is secure. I'm finished and done with low living, sight walking, small planning, smooth and ease, colourless dreams, mundane talking, cheap giving and dwarfed roles. I no longer need prosperity, position, promotion, pre-eminence or popularity. I don't have to be right, first, tops, recognised, praised, regarded or rewarded. I now live by faith, lean on His presence, walk in patience, live by prayer and labour with power. My face is set. My gate is fast. My goal is the Kingdom of God. My road is narrow. My way is rough. My companions few. My guide reliable and my mission is clear. I cannot be bought, compromised, detoured, lured away, turned back, deluded or delayed. I will not flinch in the face of sacrifice, hesitate in the presence of adversaries, negotiate at the pool of popularity or meander in the maze of mediocrity. I won't give up, shut up, let up; until I've stayed up, stored up, prayed up, paid up, spoken up for the cause of Christ. I must go until He comes, give until I drop, teach until all know, run until He stops me. I am a disciple of Jesus Christ!"

What a tremendous declaration of dedication! A church full of people like this would be all it need take to turn our community back to God. One scripture that is particularly helpful to back up such a life style is found in 2 Corinthians 5:15, here it says, *"And he died for all, that all who live might live no longer for themselves but for him who for their sake died and was raised."* This dedication to Christ is not seen so much in how loudly we sing the hymns, how many Bible verses we are able to quote, what quantity of tracts we can give out, or whether we speak in "tongues." It is seen in how we live our daily lives!

In eighteen years of ministry and travelling throughout the country, I've stayed in the homes of thousands of Christians. One of the things I find so interesting in these places are the Christian posters, texts and plaques that are displayed. Some of the best posters I've seen are found on the back of the bathroom door! In one home I stayed at, on their bathroom door, I saw a large poster and it only had a short sentence on, but that simple statement made a deep impression upon me. This is what it said, - *"Live As Though Christ Died Yesterday, Rose Today And Is Coming Back Tomorrow!"*

Having looked at the absolute necessity of, "Death to self," and considered the importance of "Dedication to Christ," there is one final part of Galatians 2:20 that we need to look at. The significance of:

Thirdly,- DEPENDENCE ON FAITH

Paul has already said, *"I have been crucified with Christ; it is no longer I who live, but Christ who lives in me."* He then goes on to say, *"and the life I now live in the flesh, I live by faith in the Son of God who loved me and gave himself for me."* This is a new dimension of living, full of unlimited potential. It is a fact of life that to a large extent, everything's potential comes out in its environment. For example, the potential of a bird comes out in the environment of the air. With the fish it is water and for the Oak tree, it is the earth. As far as every Christian is concerned though, their potential comes out in the environment of faith! This is why the Bible says, *"For we walk by faith, not by sight."* (2 Corinthians 5:7).

Our new life in Christ is governed by a brand new principle, one that is totally the reverse of how we lived before we were converted. It now depends upon a selfless, single-minded faith. Each of us start on an equal footing. The Bible says, *".... God hath dealt to every man the measure of faith."* (Romans 12:3, AV). We all have the ability to believe and depend on faith. Perhaps at times you may have been tempted to think that if you had more faith, then your life would be very different. Some people today seem to think that they need faith the size of a mountain to move the mustard seed! This is not so, because Jesus said, *".... If you have faith as small as a mustard seed, you can say to this mountain, "move from here to there" and it will move. Nothing will be impossible for you."* (Matthew 17:20&21, NIV).

The mustard seed is one of the smallest seeds that you could ever come across. If therefore, it only takes the tiniest amount of faith to achieve great things, the issue is not how much faith we've got, but what we do with the faith that we have! People live their lives with a diversity of attitudes and beliefs. Because of this they can have various kinds of faith. For instance, some people have what could be termed as:

(A) *Dormant Faith*

These people have the ability to believe God's word, but they neglect to use their faith in challenging circumstances. It lies dormant, unused and asleep in their lives. They may well say, "I've got all the faith in the world!" But that is their problem, they've still got it! They hold on to it! For faith to work, it needs to be released into God's word and into situations of need. These type of people never take any risks, they always remain where they feel safe and comfortable, quite content to allow opportunities to pass them by. For some what also causes their faith to lie dormant might be the busyness of life and various pressures that they've come under. With others, they might have become discouraged by failure and disappointment in something. As a result the faith that they have, has been allowed to become unused.

(B) *Diverted Faith*

This faith comes from people who certainly use their ability to believe, but they release their faith in the wrong direction. The problem with them is that it is misdirected and they believe the wrong things. These are the people who have a strong faith that dramatically affects their lives and achievements, but in a negative way. They find themselves believing their doubts and fears; their circumstances, their feelings and often the opinions of others over and above what God has said. When faced with the difficulties and challenges that life throws up, they believe the very things that contradict the word of God!

(C) *Divided Faith*

This is an interesting expression of faith because very often it is sincere and good, but it is a partial believing. We might find some things relatively easy to believe for and could in fact be quite strong in some areas of faith, then in others areas of our life be full of doubt and unbelief. For example, we might have no problem in believing God to answer other people's prayers, to meet their needs and to use their lives in a significant way. There may be no difficulty believing that God will bless and move through other people's ministry, but then when it comes to ourselves, and what God will do for us, we could be full of doubts.

This divided faith is seen very clearly in the Bible, with the father who had a son, afflicted by a deaf and dumb spirit. We know the parent had faith because he believed Jesus was the one who could answer the need of his child, yet at the same time he had to acknowledge areas of unbelief as well. He cries out with tears to Jesus and says, *".... Lord, I believe; help thou mine unbelief."* (Mark 9:24, AV).

What is necessary for ourselves, if we are to remain consistent, especially when faced with the problems and challenges of life, is not a Dormant, Diverted or Divided faith. God wants us to live with a **DEPENDANT FAITH** that is expressed in the words from Galatians 2:20, *".... And the life that I now live in the flesh I live by faith in the Son of God, who loved me and gave himself for me."*

The assurance of this faith and the foundation of its confidence is the centrality of the cross in our life. It is the cross which reminds us of the fact that God is for us, and we are important, indeed of great worth to Him. The cross demonstrates in unmistakable terms that God loves us deeply. The significance of this revelation of love in relation to faith is seen in the Bible when it says, *".... faith worketh by love."* (Galatians 5:6, AV), and again in the scripture, *"There is no fear in love. But perfect love drives out fear....."* (1 John 4:18, NIV). When we are secure in God's love it activates faith and stimulates confidence within us. This is what Paul was expressing when he said, *"He who did not spare his own Son but gave him up for us all, will he not also give us all things with him?"* (Romans 8:32).

The apostle was simply saying in effect, "Look it's absurd, God was prepared to go to the length of allowing His own son to die upon the cross to demonstrate the depth of His love for us. If He was willing in this way to make clear the extent of His commitment and the value of our lives to Him, then of course He will answer our prayer, honour His promises and meet all our needs through Christ Jesus!

The Lord is wanting to use powerfully those people who live with this sort of faith. He desires to do extraordinary things through those who will depend on Him. This is just what Joshua was encouraging Israel to believe when he said to them, *"Consecrate yourselves, for tomorrow the Lord will do amazing things among you."* (Joshua 3:5, NIV). It is important to see our personal responsibility. No one else can make this happen for us; not our spouse, parents, Church leader or friend. We have to consecrate "ourselves" to live the life we've spoken about throughout this book. It is then that God will honour the promise of His word and do amazing things.

As we, by faith, take the four keys that have been presented, a new dimension of consistency will be opened up to our lives. We shall remain in victory by, **Stepping beyond Sorrow; Standing in life's Storms; Grasping the dynamic power of Grace** and seeking to live by the principle of, **Christ Centred Consecration**.

Other publications by Yan Hadley are available from :

New Life In Christ Ministries
45 Heatherbrook Road
Leicester
LE4 1AL

Telephone : 0116 235 6992

REAPING GOD'S HARVEST
(Equipping The Church For Evangelism)

Yan's aim in this book is to stimulate faith in the lives of every believer to discover the ability of sharing Christ with others. Through clear practical teaching and personal illustrations evangelism is seen to be, not only a responsibility, but also a privilege and joy.

ANSWERING TODAY'S PROBLEMS
(Helping ourselves to help others)

This book shows clearly God's answer to some common problems in life today. People will find help not only for themselves, but also insight into being able to help others. Some of the aspects covered are:

- Tackling anxiety and worry.
- Letting go of resentment.
- Rising up from discouragement.
- Overcoming insecurity.
- Guidance in uncertainty.
- Finding hope in depression.
- Release from guilt.